Studies and Melodious Etudes for Clarinet

by

Robert Lowry
in collaboration with
James Ployhar

To The Teacher

"Studies And Melodious Etudes", Level II, is a supplementary technic book of the Belwin "STUDENT INSTRUMENTAL COURSE". Although planned as a companion and correlating book to the method, "The Clarinet Student", it can also be used effectively with most intermediate clarinet instruction books. It provides for extended and additional treatment in technical areas, which are limited in the basic method because of lack of space. Emphasis is on developing musicianship through scales, warm-ups and technical drills, musicianship studies and interesting melody-like etudes.

The Belwin "STUDENT INSTRUMENTAL COURSE" - A course for individual and class instruction of LIKE instruments, at three levels, for all band instruments.

EACH BOOK IS COMPLETE IN ITSELF BUT ALL BOOKS ARE CORRELATED WITH EACH OTHER

METHOD
"The B♭ Clarinet Student"
For individual
or
class instruction.

ALTHOUGH EACH BOOK CAN BE USED SEPARATELY, IDEALLY, ALL SUPPLEMENTARY BOOKS SHOULD BE USED AS COMPANION BOOKS WITH THE METHOD

STUDIES & MELODIOUS ETUDES	TUNES FOR TECHNIC	B♭ CLARINET SOLOS	DUETS FOR STUDENTS
Supplementary scales, warm-up and technical drills, musicianship studies and melody-like etudes, all carefully correlated with the method.	Technical type melodies, variations, and "famous passages" from musical literature for the development of — technical dexterity.	Four separate correlated Solos, with piano accompaniment, written or arranged by Robert Lowry: Cavelleria Rusticana...*Masagni* The Sioux Song and Dance.................... *Lowry* Valse and Volante...... *Lowry* Song and Prayer from "Hansel and Gretel"..*Humperdinck*	A book of carefully correlated duet arrangements of interesting and familiar melodies without piano accompaniments. Available for: Flute B♭ Clarinet Alto Sax B♭ Cornet Trombone

CLARINET FINGERING CHART

How To Read The Chart

● - Indicates hole closed, or keys to be pressed.

○ - Indicates hole open.

When a number is given, refer to the picture of the Clarinet for additional key to be pressed.

When two notes are given together (F♯ and G♭), they are the same tone and, of course, played the same way.

When there are two or more fingerings given for a note, use the first one unless your teacher tells you otherwise.

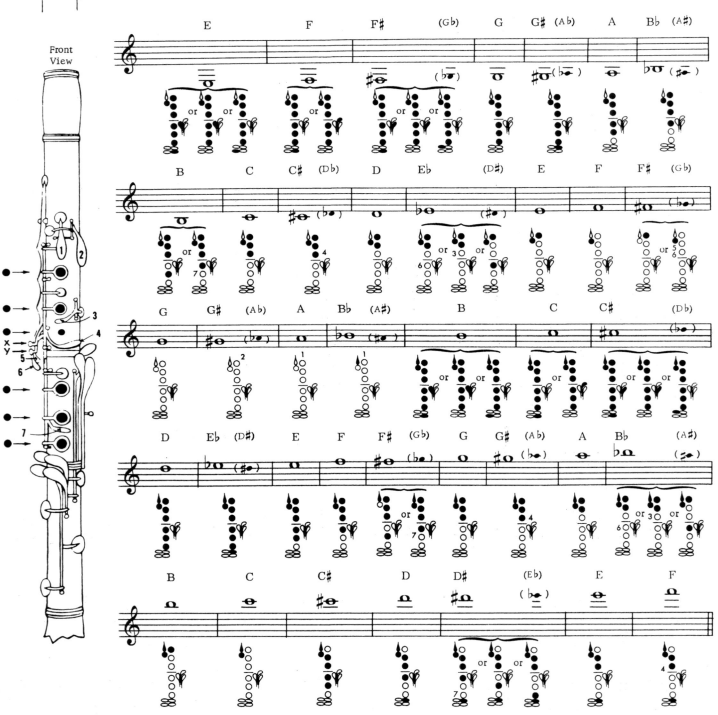

These Studies and Etudes will compliment and correlate with the method book "THE CLARINET STUDENT" Level II (Intermediate).

C Major Studies

Be careful to keep the tempo steady when making the dynamic changes.

Etude No. 1

4

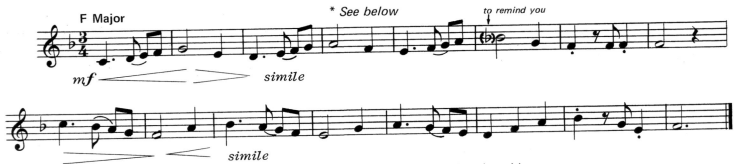

F Major

See below

to remind you

mf — simile

* Remember to play the "A" Key with the side of your index finger at the first knuckle.

G Major

to remind you

Etude No. 2

Maestoso (majestically)

Don't lose time at the double bar lines.

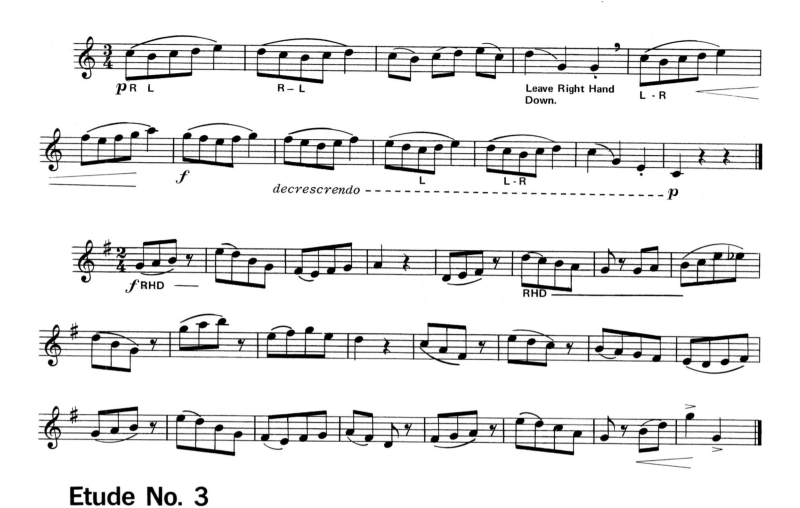

Etude No. 3

A general rule for more musical interest is to crescendo slightly when a passage ascends . . . decrescendo if it descends. Try it on this Etude.

6

ff – 1st. time pp – 2nd. time

Play this type of grace note quickly and just before the beat. Make the grace notes "graceful" and don't allow them to sound like "finger accidents".

Etude No. 4

D.C. al Fine

B.I.C.207

Recall the smoother chromatic fingering for B♮ and F♯.

A star (*) will indicate where the chromatic fingering is best to use.

Use the chromatic fingering for all F♯'s.

Etude No. 5

For better tone and intonation on the higher notes, remember to firm the embouchure to the very "peak of the pitch" and push the air faster (more breath support).

Stately (In a slow two)

SYNCOPATION — *A long note, or notes, between two shorter notes.*   Notice that the tongue action *(articulation)* is identical to the line above.

For Speed

Etude No. 6

Andante (moderately slow)

— Tone — Air support from Belly
— Dynamics — Shape the line

Review the smoother chromatic fingering for F#.

continue for speed

continue for speed

Use chromatic F#- Gb fingerings unless indicated otherwise.

Etude No. 7

Alla Breve (¢) compared to 2/4

Both lines should sound the same.

The eighth note gets one beat.

Etude No. 8

A *CHROMATIC SCALE* is one that progresses in half steps. It is without a doubt the most important of all scales to know well. Make certain that you are using the correct chromatic fingerings. Memorize it and play it regularly in each practice session with various articulations.

Articulation Examples

Etude No. 9

A minor *(Harmonic Form)*

For Speed

Etude No. 10

Two measures of 3/8 time are the same as one measure of 6/8.

Andante in A minor

For Speed

Adagio (very slow)

Etude No. 11

Repeat this Etude until you can do it **Presto** (fast).

G Major

C Major

RHD

We will now study three new notes. These are in the *ALTISSIMO* (high) register and are much easier if related to the CLARION register. In the following studies, the upper note will respond by lifting the first finger of the left hand . . and by adding a bit more speed to the air stream.

To make a smoother slur, the experienced clarinetist learns to roll or pivot the first finger down and away from the tone hole rather than to abruptly lift the finger. Try it.

Leave the Eb key down for both notes.

* *Leave the Eb key down.*

Chromatic Study

Etude No. 12

Tempo di Valse

Practice so that you can feel this Etude in one beat to the bar.

mp *Tongue Legato (smooth) unless marked otherwise.*

D minor (harmonic form)

Syncopation Study

For Speed

Slowly — for good tone.

pp - 1st. time
ff - 2nd. time

Etude No. 13

For more musical interest, crescendo when the melodic line ascends; diminuendo when the line descends.

Adagio (slow) — in D♭ minor

mf

RHD

ritard- - - - - - - - - - -

16

For better intonation, remember to keep your little finger on the E♭ Key for D and higher notes.

D minor

Etude No. 14

Slow and Stately

Continue same style.

B.I.C.207

E minor (harmonic form)

Etude No. 15

Andante in E minor

Remember to crescendo as the melodic line ascends and vice-versa.

Etude No. 16

Bb Major Scale — MEMORIZE

E minor

For Speed

D minor — In a slow 3.

Etude No. 17

Review the 1/1 fingering for high Bb.

Andante

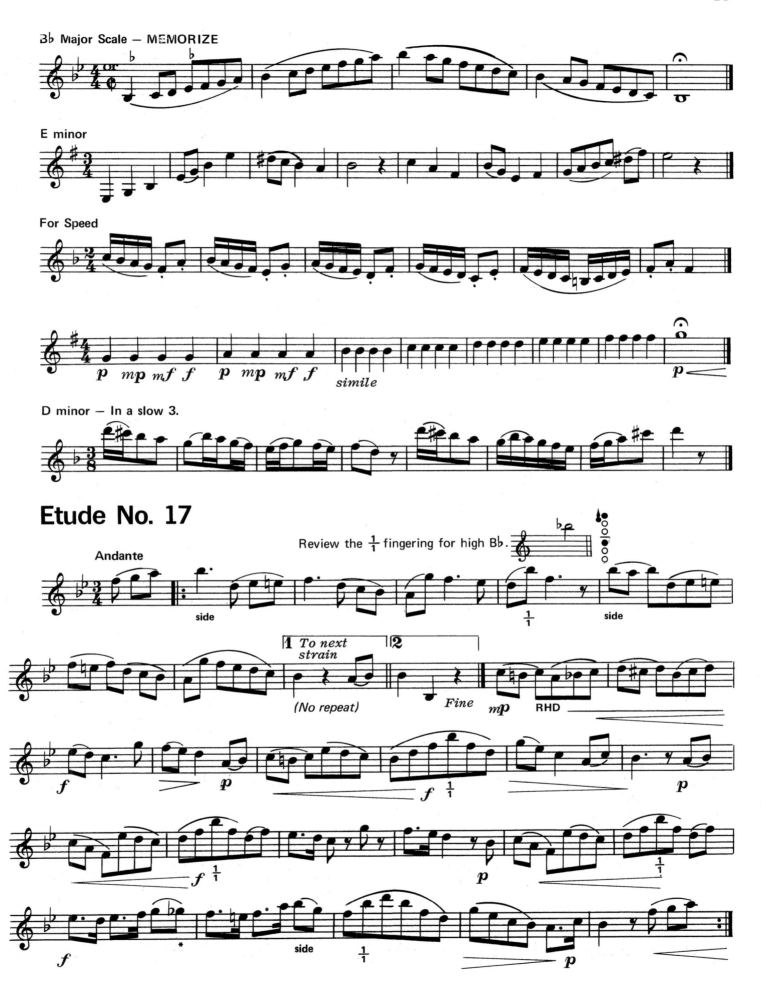

Perhaps you have noticed that Bb $\begin{array}{c}\text{♭o}\end{array}$ is a bit thin and fuzzy compared to other notes? We do have a fingering that

gives us a better tone and intonation. It should be used *at all times* for Bb *unless* the note preceding or following it needs the right hand fingers.

Here is the best tonal fingering for Bb. Play "A" and add the third side key *(the one above Key 5)* in place of the register key. It is known as the *"side"* fingering. This key should be contacted near the first knuckle of the right index finger without getting your other fingers out of a normal position.

Etude No. 18

Spiritoso (with spirit)

D Major Scale — MEMORIZE

Etude No. 19

Fast march tempo

If the wide intervals gave you trouble on the Etude, refer back to Page 14.

B.I.C.207

Etude No. 20

Waltz in D Major

G minor *(Harmonic Form)*

Fast 6/8 (In a moderate two)

These lines should sound identical in rhythm.

E minor

Make certain that the eighth notes are even after playing triplets.

Etude No. 21

Maestoso in G minor

Largo (very slow)

Remember to add a faster stream of air and firm the embouchure a bit more for a better tone and intonation on the higher notes.

In a fast 6

These lines should not sound the same rhythmically.

Keep the same tempo on both lines.

RHD

A minor

Etude No. 22

Slow march tempo

Use side B♭ fingerings.

reg.   reg.

1 reg.

No Repeat — Go right on

2 reg.   *Fine*   side

reg.   side

reg.   side   side

D. C. al Fine

B minor (harmonic form)

Attention to articulations

Syncopation in E minor

f - 1st. time
p - 2nd. time

Use side B♭ fingerings.

In two

% means to repeat the previous measure.

Etude No. 23

Moderato in B minor

side A#'s

a tempo

ritard

accelerando [faster] - *rallentondo*

fork B

26

Etude No. 24

Work towards a fast four.

Fine

[repeat to beginning]

B.I.C.207

Eb Major Scale — MEMORIZE

For Speed

In Eb Major, we encounter a rather awkward interval to finger. (High Ab to Bb) The fingers must coordinate perfectly for a clean result. The following studies will help you solve the problem.

Repeat each measure four times.

Etude No. 25

Andante

RHD

In two

pp 1st. time
ff 2nd. time

Marcato

f

mf R - L   R - L - R - L   L   R   L - R   L - R - L - R

Etude No. 26

The articulations are especially important in this Waltz Etude.

Andante Cantabile (in a flowing style)

mf

f

A Major Scale — MEMORIZE

Slowly in A minor

Etude No. 27
Flowing (one beat per measure)

D.C. al Fine

Notice the rhythmic sameness between three eighth notes in $\frac{9}{8}$ time and triplets in $\frac{3}{4}$ time.

Etude No. 28

March tempo

Go right on
p *[last time only]*
Fine

D.C. al Fine

Ab Major Scale — MEMORIZE

Etude No. 29

Remember to alternate (R-L or L-R) with the little fingers. Don't slide!

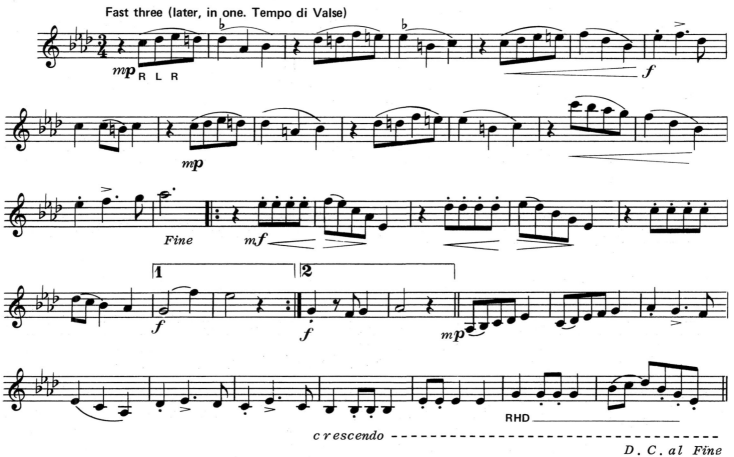

crescendo -

D. C. al Fine

B.I.C.207

SUMMARY OF COMMONLY USED MAJOR SCALES AND THEIR RELATIVE MINORS.

Memorize and play with various articulations.